Global Warming

Susan Philip

Global Warming
New Horizon Media ©

First Edition: December 2007
64 Pages
Printed in India.

ISBN 978-81-8368-619-8
Pro-ya-en - 3

Prodigy Books
177/103, First Floor,
Ambal's Building, Lloyds Road,
Royapettah, Chennai 600 014.
Ph: +91-44-4200-9603

Email : support@nhm.in
Website : www.nhm.in

All rights relating to this work rest with the copyright holder. Except for reviews and quotations, use or republication of any part of this work is prohibited under the copyright act, without the prior written permission of the publisher of this book.

Chapter 1
The Disappearing Cap

I'm starving... I must get food. I must get it soon... No, that's not a child like you thinking aloud. That's a huge animal which stands up and shakes himself, before lumbering forward. He is a polar bear, living in the Arctic Circle. Let's call him Nanuq, the Eskimo word for polar bear. Nanuq has been asleep on an ice-floe–a large chunk of floating ice–on the Arctic Ocean. He has been feeding on seals and walruses through the winter months. He has grown enormous in the process.

But now it's spring, it's getting warmer. And Nanuq is finding that food is harder to get.

The huge stretch of white we see in pictures of the North Pole is just ice–not land. It is a massive, slowly-moving cap on the top of the world, and the ice-floes that break off from it are the hunting bases of the polar bears. Nanuq and the other bears of his species are strong swimmers, move from ice-floe to ice-floe and catch their prey from the ocean. But the ice has been shrinking. The edge of the cap has been getting farther from the land, and the floes have also been drifting farther apart, meaning that the bears have to swim longer distances, sometimes too long.

Nanuq is surprised and confused when he finds he can't see where the next ice-floe is. He plunges into the water anyway, bracing against the piercing cold and starts swimming. He is a big bear, so he manages, after swimming for miles, to find another floating chunk of ice, and clambers on, shaking with weakness. His extra-efficient nose soon picks up the scent of a seal in the sea beneath, and, using the last of his strength, Nanuq digs through the ice and drags his prey up. Food at last!

But not all polar bears are as lucky as Nanuq, particularly females with young cubs. They're weaker because they have had to feed their cubs throughout the winter months which they spend in dens they dig on land. People who study wildlife are finding that many adult females and cubs drown before they can find food.

Polar bears are in danger because their territory is disappearing. The ice on which they depend for life is literally melting away, because the earth is heating up. This is a phenomenon which the scientists call Global Warming.

Chapter 2

All Wrapped Up

So what exactly is this global warming which is destroying Nanuq's home?

You'd be surprised to know that it has been around for millions of years.

Imagine that it's a cold, damp, dark, rainy day. What would you like to do best? Huddle under a warm blanket, obviously. You'll find yourself becoming nice and comfortable before long, and you might even drift off to sleep.

Well, our Earth has been cuddling under a blanket almost all its life. This blanket has been keeping the Earth warm-in other words, it is responsible for global warming.

As you know, the Earth is constantly moving along its own orbit around the sun in space. Space is an unimaginably cold and dark place, while the sun is HOT. If it hadn't been for this blanket covering the Earth, you and I would not exist today. Life, as we know it, would not have been able to survive, as, by day the Earth would have got unbearably hot because of the heat and light sent out by the sun, and by night, it would have quickly become bitterly cold, since all the heat would have bounced back into space.

Actually, Mars is a planet quite like Earth in the Solar System, but it doesn't have this comforting blanket, and so it's freezing cold. Too cold for life.

This blanket is actually the layer of air around the Earth, which we call atmosphere. The atmosphere is made up of various gases, the most important of which is oxygen, or O_2, because we need oxygen to live. But other gases also play a part in preserving life. Some of them filter the heat and light of the sun during the day, so that the Earth doesn't get unbearably hot, and, at night they prevent a lot of the heat from escaping into space. So the Earth doesn't get too hot or too cold, it's just right, like the porridge which Goldilocks ate from Baby Bear's bowl.

In cold places, there's often snow and frost in winter, and tender plants are damaged, sometimes even killed. So people build sheds made of glass and use them to shelter plants which can't take the cold weather. The glass allows the light and heat from the sun to enter, and traps the heat inside, keeping the shed warm. Such sheds are called Greenhouses, and scientists have used this system to describe the function of the blanket of air surrounding the Earth. They call it the Greenhouse Effect.

But too much of a good thing can be bad. What if you put on flannel pyjamas, two sweaters, a wind cheater, a muffler, a monkey cap, thick woollen socks and gloves, and then cover yourself with a blanket on a rainy day? You'd soon find yourself sweating and uncomfortable, wouldn't you? That's because you don't really need so much warm clothing.

Something like that is happening to the world today. The blanket around the Earth is getting thicker. More and more heat, much more than needed, is getting trapped, as it is not able to escape into space, and many forms of life here are beginning to feel uncomfortably hot.

So you see, while the blanket of air which warms the globe is very important for life on this Earth, it should be of just the right thickness, otherwise we're in trouble. The Greenhouse Effect, which was originally a good, life-sustaining function, has come to have a negative meaning. When scientists use the term now, they usually mean that something harmful is going on.

You'll have an idea of how serious the problem is if you remember that Venus, another planet in our Solar System, is like Father Bear's porridge–TOO HOT–because it has an extremely thick gas blanket around it, too thick for life to survive.

Let's go back to the North Pole for a quick look at Nanuq. Like all polar bears, he's got TWO coats of fur, not one, and a very thick layer of blubber, as the fat on the bodies of animals in extreme cold conditions is called. He needs these to protect him from the terrible cold of the Arctic winters. And in summer, which is never hot in that part of the world, his body uses some of the stored fat to survive on days when he doesn't get enough food. So he was managing to stay reasonably cool. But now, the ice in his territory is melting, the temperature is rising. Poor

Nanuq! He must be feeling a little like you would be if you had put on all those warm clothes and got under your blanket.

What is making the Earth unnecessarily warm is the build up of gases in the atmosphere. These gases are known as Greenhouse Gases.

Chapter 3

Just Gas

OK, so let's talk about gas.

Did I just hear someone say *YUCK*?

No, we're not going to talk of the kind of gas the doctor prescribes an antacid for, nor the sort that comes in the cylinder your mom uses in the kitchen. Not even the gas the man at the fun-fair uses to fill the bright balloons that bring a smile to your face and then tears to your eyes as you watch them float up in the sky.

The gases that we're going to talk about now are floating about in the atmosphere.

Let's take a closer look at Earth's own special blanket. It is a combination of many gases.

The biggest ingredients are Nitrogen (N_2) and Oxygen (O_2). Oxygen, as we know, is what our bodies keep when we breathe air in, and without oxygen, we would all die. It makes up 21 percent of the atmosphere, while there's a lot more of nitrogen around–78 percent in fact. The remaining one percent is made up of several other gases, including the ones collectively known as the greenhouse gases. They're the ones we're interested in at the moment.

The greenhouse gases are mainly water vapour, carbon dioxide, methane, nitrous oxide and ozone.

What do these gases actually do to make a difference to life?

Basically, they filter radiant heat–a combination of heat and light–from the sun, acting like an umbrella over the Earth so that it doesn't fall directly on the planet. Just as importantly, they absorb the infrared rays that are reflected back from the Earth. Infrared literally means below red, with red being the colour of visible light. That means they absorb the invisible light, or, in other words, the heat that stops short of turning into a glow, transmitted from the surface of the Earth. (The Earth is cooler than the sun of course, and so isn't hot enough to turn the heat bouncing back from it into light.) These infrared rays are absorbed better by the greenhouse gases. Some of this reflected heat is released into space while some of it is bounced back to Earth, creating a fine balance in temperature.

Most of the greenhouse gases are in that part of the atmosphere that is closer to the Earth, known as the troposphere. Ozone is mainly found in an upper layer of the atmosphere, called the stratosphere, and plays a slightly different role. It traps heat and blocks harmful ultraviolet rays from the sun.

The bigwigs of the atmosphere–Nitrogen and Oxygen–are not greenhouse gases because they don't have the property of absorbing or emitting infrared rays. That great task is the duty of this one percent group. Great to know that you may be small, but can still make a huge difference, isn't it?

The greenhouse gases evolved with the Earth. Volcanic eruptions when the Earth was being born might have put a lot of them, carbon dioxide, for instance, into the atmosphere. A cycle is kept up when we breathe in oxygen and give out carbon dioxide and plants do the reverse. Carbon dioxide is also produced by combustion–which means, it is generated when we burn things. Methane is given out by microbes–tiny organisms–that live in wet, muddy places including paddy fields. It is also released by cattle (Oops! No antacid for the cow!). And believe it or not, by termites–yes, those little insects that bore into wood and destroy your furniture and your door frames.

But now, the amount of greenhouse gases in the atmosphere is increasing. This has set off a vicious cycle. For instance, most scientists agree that Nanuq's homeland is vanishing mainly because global warming is changing from a life-nurturing function into a life-threatening one. And the melting ice is itself turning up the heat. The blinding white wastes of the Poles reflect some of the heat of the sun back to space much as a mirror does, and reduce the radiant heat on Earth to an extent. But now, there's less heat being bounced off because of fewer icy surfaces. So more heat is being absorbed by the oceans, which in turn melts more ice. And so it goes on. In Nature, every little bit adds up to something. In this case it's global warming. No wonder Nanuq had to swim for miles before he found an ice-floe to hunt from.

Scientists say we humans are responsible for upsetting nature's delicate balance of greenhouse gases. We have adopted lifestyles that are generating more and more greenhouse gases which nature had earlier put into the atmosphere. We are even adding some new ones to the list!

Chapter 4

Life In A Gas Factory

We just saw that the main greenhouse gases are water vapour, carbon dioxide, methane, nitrous oxide and ozone. We found out that a lot of it was put there by nature in a certain proportion, for a certain purpose–that of regulating the Earth's temperature and protecting it from harmful ultraviolet rays from the sun.

We also saw that scientists feel the quantity of greenhouse gases is increasing because of the way we humans are using the Earth and its resources. We've turned the world into a virtual gas factory.

Let's pretend we're a flock of birds, flying away from the cold winter to warmer lands. We pass over a great many countries, and what do we see?

We see buildings, buildings and more buildings everywhere. The older birds in our flock remember a time when the land below us had a lot of green, and when they were tired from long hours of flying, they could just swoop down and settle on trees. When they were rested, they would flutter their wings and take off again, falling easily into formation, and following their leader. But now, we see very little green. When we want to rest, we have to search for suitable roosting places, and they're not easy to find because buildings fill the landscape. In fact, sometimes it's hard to even see what's below us, because there's smoke and smog lying over everything–thick, black smoke rising from factory chimneys, smoke spilling from vehicle exhaust pipes, fog drifting in from the seas and waterways, thickened by black emissions from various types of water transport.

Trees are being cut wherever possible to make room for more buildings, as populations expand and there's more need for housing and factories to produce all kinds of goods. It's no fun being a migrating bird in such conditions, so let's come down to Earth and continue exploring the subject of global warming.

Various groups of scientists who have been studying weather and climate over the years have noticed, that ever since the Industrial Revolution, the Earth's temperature has been rising much faster than it was doing earlier. The Industrial Revolution refers to a period in the 18th century when industries sprang up all over Europe and the Western world in general, spurred by new discoveries in science and technology, like the invention of the steam engine and the electric bulb. Factories making a whole range of products, from machinery to textiles, and from chocolates to cutlery, grew up almost overnight.

Now, factories need fuel of some sort, be it wood or coal or oil or electricity. Most of the world's energy comes from fossil fuels–fuel which is generated from burning substances like coal, petrol and natural gas which have been formed by the remains of dead animals lying buried far underground for millions and millions of years. This is combustion, which, as we saw earlier, releases carbon dioxide into the air. The more fuel we burn, the more carbon dioxide is generated.

Then there are the vehicles. Here in India, your grandparents or great grandparents may remember a time when a car was considered a luxury and a symbol of wealth and power. They will tell you how a motor car chugging slowly and majestically along a road would attract an audience all along the way. Boys and girls would run beside the vehicle, shouting with excitement, and even grown men and women would leave their chores to stop and stare at the rare sight. But today, there's so much traffic on the roads that pedestrians are fast becoming an endangered species! The majority of people living in towns and cities are now able to afford a vehicle of some sort, and a growing number of families have more than one. But there's a price to pay. These vehicles are polluting the atmosphere, sending more carbon dioxide up.

To add to the problem, as we already saw, trees are being cut down to make room for factories and houses, so there's less of vegetation around to absorb the carbon dioxide and release the oxygen we need. So there's further imbalance, and the extra carbon dioxide drifts up into the atmosphere and adds to the thickness of the Earth's blanket.

Methane generation is also going up. Agricultural areas in the developing world, as well as cattle-breeding areas are big sources. Some studies show that an average cow releases as much as 280 litres of Methane every day!

Oil drilling and mining activities also send out methane, and the concentration of this gas has been going up by roughly 1 percent each year.

As for nitrous oxide, fossil fuels are the culprit again, as well as fertilizers.

Then there's Ozone. Just as ozone plays two roles as a greenhouse gas–blocking harmful rays and absorbing heat–there are also two layers of ozone–the gas in the stratosphere, as well as what is floating around closer to Earth. The stratosphere is where nature placed Ozone, and where it has a positive role to play. Strangely, some of the fruits of our technological advancement, refrigerators, for instance, are actually harming this ozone, destroying it and letting in ultraviolet rays, which is affecting human health. Plus, more radiant heat is able to get in and warm the waters, melt the ice and so forth. The ozone that is closer home is what we send up ourselves. These form when something known as volatile organic compounds, we'll call them VOCs for short, combine with nitrogen oxide in the air. Now VOCs come from many sources–some as ordinary as paint thinner and furniture polish.

Nitrogen oxides are mainly released during combustion. But they need a third party to produce ozone–sunlight.

So, the pollutant VOCs mix with Nitrogen oxides in the presence of sunlight to make ozone which is harmful to human health. The ozone itself sometimes combines with other pollutants in the air to form smog. Remember when you were a bird flying off to a warm country?

So that's another greenhouse gas which is not acting the way nature planned.

Besides, our industries and other activities have added some compounds containing a substance called fluorine to the atmosphere, and increased the negative type of greenhouse effect.

Water vapour, which makes up the biggest chunk of the greenhouse gases, is not directly affected by human activity. But as the Earth grows warmer, the world's water bodies are heating up. In the North Pole, Nanuq's ice is melting, and more evaporation is happening. So water vapour is also building up in the atmosphere.

Phew! It's getting warmer, isn't it?

Chapter 5

Blowing Hot and Cold

Yes, as we were saying, it's getting hotter.

But is this a new experience for the Earth? Not really. Scientists have told us that the Earth was an icy cold place to begin with. Gradually, over millions of years, the greenhouse gases evolved, the Earth stopped shivering, temperature started to go up, it became warm enough to support some life.

Still, massive areas of the Earth were under ice. Gradually, it warmed further, a lot of ice melted, it became warmer still, and more forms of life developed. The species of living creatures that came up in the different parts of the world were geared to the climate of that area. They developed characteristics or abilities that helped them to cope with the temperatures of that place, and survive.

But the Earth's climate did not remain stable. The glaciers started playing a game of advance and retreat, acting like kabaddi players in slow motion. First they'd draw back, exposing more land on one hand, and putting other stretches of land under water (because drawing back meant melting, which added more water to the oceans and seas, which in turn submerged low-lying areas). Then the mercury would dip and glaciers would drift forward, changing land and sea patterns once more. Of course, this did not happen every year, or even every hundred years, it took many thousands of years to happen. The process was extremely slow and the effects or changes were equally gradual, so gradual that they were hardly noticed. But there was a pattern.

Weathermen called the hot and cold phases glacial periods and inter-glacial periods. The inter-glacial periods were the warm times.

As the cycle went on, and one phase followed another, life forms underwent changes too. Animals migrated in search of more habitable places when the climate in the areas where they were living changed too much for comfort. Sometimes they succeeded, sometimes they adapted, and sometimes they couldn't cope and gave up the battle. We all know dinosaurs flourished on Earth at one time. They rolled in play on sunny grasslands and stalked the depths of steamy jungles. And then they vanished. Like the gentle Brontosaurus and the menacing Tyrannosaurus Rex, many animals became extinct. Climate Change is among the main accused.

So we see, the Earth has been blowing hot and cold ever since it was born. This age we're living in is an inter-glacial one. Meaning, it's generally warm.

If then it is normal, and even expected, for the Earth's temperatures to dip and rise at regular intervals, what's all this hype about global warming now, you might ask.

There are two views, broadly speaking, about global warming. One set of people, including some scientists, feel that the Earth is acting very much in character. Humans had nothing to do with earlier shifts from glacial to inter-glacial periods and back again–in fact, till very recently (from the point of view of the Earth's age), humans didn't even exist! There were no humans when the dinosaur lived, and if climate change was one of the reasons they became extinct, mankind can't be held responsible. Warming and cooling happened in predictable succession without any help from us. So we have nothing to do but move with the times now. That's one school of thought.

Those who support this theory say people are getting unnecessarily alarmed, and the correlation seen between human activity and rising temperatures is not scientifically proven.

On the other side of the debate are people, including scientists, environmentalists and thinkers, who say that our lifestyles are definitely having an impact on climate. They predict that, based on present data, temperatures are sure to go up much higher if people don't work as one to prevent it. And the consequences will be disastrous.

Whose side should we be on?

To decide, we need to know if anything is different about the climate changes that are now taking place, as compared to those that happened in the early years of the Earth's history.

Well, there is a difference.

There is no dispute about the fact that the Earth is getting hotter. People on both sides of the argument agree that temperatures are going up. What they don't agree about is whether humans are responsible for that or not.

What scientists have found is that though a cyclical rise in temperature is normal and expected, what is different this time is the extent of the rise.

Scientists use various methods to work out the temperature patterns from early days, conducting studies on rocks, fossils and even tree rings to get a picture of what the climate was like in distant days, both before human beings evolved and after the birth of civilization. An important fact they noticed is that temperature had risen or fallen very slowly and very slightly. For example, 15,000 years ago, most of Europe and the North American continent were covered with sheets of ice. This was known as the Ice Age. Then, ever so slowly, over hundreds and hundreds of years, this ice cover was drawn back. The landscape changed, wildlife adapted. After about 5000 years, scientists and historians tell us, life had spread out significantly on these continents, and flourished. Nothing happened overnight.

Within the glacial and inter-glacial periods themselves, scientists say there are less dramatic changes. These occur at shorter intervals. During the 14th Century, for example, there was a period when temperatures dropped–this was called the Little Ice Age, and the whole of Europe was shivering in the cold. The concern then was Global Cooling, not Global Warming. But suddenly, the barometers started soaring again.

Over the last couple of centuries, however, the hike in temperature has been rapid. In the last hundred years, the average temperature of the Earth has gone up by 1 degree C.

One degree? All this fuss over just a one-degree rise? I hear you ask. Well, just think about this–during the Ice Age, when there was hardly any life, the Earth's average temperature was just about 5 degrees cooler than it is now. That should give you an idea of how important each degree on the barometer is, whether it goes up or down. And the present one-degree hike has already made a marked difference to the lives of some of those with whom we share this Earth. Ask Nanuq in the North Pole. At one time, not so very long ago, Nanuq and his friends had nothing to fear except man, and even that fear went away once governments moved to protect them. But now they have to fear nature, because they aren't being given time to adapt to changing climatic and other rhythms.

It is the speed with which the air is heating up that makes the majority of scientists sure that men have something to do with it.

The most likely catalyst–that's something that quickens change–for global warming is the increasing amount of greenhouse gases being generated by human activity. It has been argued that carbon dioxide, methane and the rest make up only a tiny quantity of the greenhouse gases. Most of it is water vapour, and as we saw earlier, man's activities haven't been producing any of this. But water vapour doesn't stay very long in the atmosphere, though it keeps getting restocked. On the other hand, carbon dioxide, methane and other greenhouse gases stick around for ages. They're like stubborn stains on the blanket, which take many washes to get rid of. So the effect of these other greenhouse gases is greater.

It has been proved that the levels of gases like carbon dioxide have gone up a great deal over the last hundred years or so, much more than the percentage of increase in the past. It is logical to say that the reason for this jump is the burning of much, much higher amounts of fossil fuels than before, to provide for man's huge need for fuel and energy.

Of course, man's role in global warming hasn't been proved beyond a shadow of doubt. But while scientists blow hot and cold on the subject, like the Earth itself, can we afford to sit back and wait for the verdict before we do something to reduce the greenhouse effect? We've already seen what is happening to Nanuq. But are only the Polar Regions at risk? Could things go wrong with the rest of the world if global warming is allowed to proceed unchecked at this pace or even faster?

What's going to happen to you and me while the experts debate?

Chapter 6

What's Cooking?

Okay, everyone's agreed that the Earth's temperature is rising in general.

What happens when things get hotter?

Heat is an agent of change. When we heat water, it boils. When we add rice to that water, the rice gets hot and it gets cooked. If we heat milk, it boils. If we allow it to continue boiling without reducing the flame, it will boil over (and we'll probably get a scolding and be made to clean up the stove as well!). If we heat bread it will become toast, and if we continue to heat it, it will become burnt toast! If we heat a plastic bowl over direct fire, it will melt and then we're in real deep trouble.

So when things get hot we should expect a change, and when things get hotter than they were meant to, the change may not be following nature's plan. If a hen warms an egg under her, it will hatch into a chick. If you put an egg into a hot oven, it will cook!

Therefore, when the Earth's temperature is going up, and going up unusually fast, we should expect changes. Let's start at the top–yes, at the North Pole–back to Nanuq's home.

Now we know that the polar ice is melting. What happens when you leave a cube of ice on a plate on the table? It melts, right? And then what happens? It turns to water. To understand what's happening to our world when ice at the poles and on mountains melts and turns into water, let's do a simple experiment.

Take a dinner plate with a raised edge (ask permission first). Stick some bits of thermocol on to the plate–if you're good with your hands, you can cut out shapes of the continents, and add little bits here and there for islands. Otherwise, just random bits of thermocol would do, some big, some small, to represent land masses and islands.

Pour water into the plate, so that it comes up to the edges of the thermocol pieces. Then place some ice cubes on the plate, on top of the thermocol if you like, and watch what happens. After a while, the ice will start melting. This will send up the level of water in the plate. The rising water will flow over parts of the thermocol, and soon, the smaller 'islands' will be submerged.

Something like that is happening on the Earth now.

As the glaciers and polar ice are melting, the volume of water is going up. This will have what is known as a ripple effect. Have you ever thrown a stone into a pond? I'm sure you have, at one time or other. Do you remember what happened? The stone would have sunk, but you would have seen circles of water widening out from the point where it struck the surface of the pond, one circle following another in an ever-expanding sequence. That's called the ripple effect. One action or event causes a reaction and that reaction causes another which again sets off one more reaction, and so on.

The most obvious and immediate result of more water in the seas and oceans is erosion. That means, the sea comes further and further up the coast (remember your world on a plate?) and each wave takes away with it a tiny bit of earth. Multiply that tiny bit of earth by thousands of waves that hit the coast, and multiply that by days, then weeks, months, a year and so on. It adds up to quite a bit of land lost, doesn't it?

We will soon have to redraw the maps of the world, because the landmasses are changing, coastlines are being eaten away, beaches have shrunk, islands have vanished.

There's also a greater danger of floods. Because rivers and streams are already getting extra water from melting ice, and during the rainy season they overflow their banks very quickly. There are flash floods, which leave no time for people to move themselves and their property to safety, or just floods, which can be very damaging to life, crops and property too. Dams are breached, bridges swept away, and death and destruction follow.

Added to that, there's the issue of heating. The cover of greenhouse gases is heating the water as well as the land on Earth. You can try a small experiment to observe this effect:

Take a small bowl of water at room temperature. Place it on a windowsill in direct sunlight. Keep a barometer near it and note down the temperature. Then take a glass bowl bigger than your bowl of water, and cover both the bowl of water and the barometer. Wait for five minutes, then read the temperature on the barometer through the glass. You'll find that it has gone up. Then lift the glass bowl and dip your little finger in the bowl of water. You'll find that it has warmed slightly. That's what's happening to our world and its water bodies because of the thickening cover of greenhouse gases.

When water increases in volume and temperature, its energy levels also change. This could lead to a whole host of problems, some of which can be felt immediately while some will bring long-term changes. There are some problems that are minor, and others that can be very dangerous.

When the energy level of water goes up, currents become stronger; they may even change direction. Warm currents and cold ones, as you know, influence weather a great deal. Rainfall in various parts of the world depends on warm currents. When currents change, weather patterns change too.

So when weather patterns change, many things will have to change as well. There will be droughts on one hand and floods on the other. Agriculture will be the most immediately affected sector, because plants need certain climatic conditions to thrive. If a region is known for a particular crop which is dependent on heavy rainfall while it is germinating and a hot dry spell while it is ripening, and there's a change in the pattern, that crop is sure to fail.

When crops fail, there will be scarcity of food, sometimes even famine.

Another effect of changes in currents and weather patterns will be an increase in both the frequency and intensity of cyclones and storms. These are familiar dangers facing seafarers, coastal cities, towns and villages. The storms will get rougher. We see that happening already. Not only that, places which were not normally prone to cyclones and storms are being battered by them. Hurricanes have caused extensive damage in many countries in the recent past, including Asia, the USA and the Middle East.

We humans are reasonably familiar with storms, cyclones, and other types of rough weather, and know what to expect. But the tsunami came to us out of the blue, didn't it? Many of us didn't even know the word till 26 December 2005. The towering, seething, rolling, speeding wall of water caught so many countries totally unawares, and we're still coping with the trauma. Even a tsunami, scientists say, can be linked to changing climate patterns, and global warming.

While a tsunami may be described as a giant wave, there are other, smaller ripples, tiny in comparison, caused by increasing water levels, but these are important too.

More water may mean good news for people in water-starved places like Chennai. But more water also means more disease. Pests like mosquitoes breed more, epidemics like malaria, cholera, typhoid and leptospirosis become frequent and fierce. The outbreak of vector-borne diseases can include some which were not known outside the pages of medical text books. Over the past couple of years, many parts of India have been reeling under chikungunya, a disease spread by a particular type of mosquito. There was almost no earlier instance of the disease in India within living memory.

Health authorities are stretched to their limits coping with such problems, and governments are spending huge amounts of money to cope with the effects of natural disasters and to help the affected people. This leaves less money to be spent on development, and on improving the quality of life. More ripples, you see?

Warmer water also affects the life forms that grow in it. Algae, which are a big source of food for fish, are at risk, and so in turn, the fish are at risk. Fewer fish mean less food for humans.

The change in weather patterns will put at risk the fragile forest and swamp areas, and destroy many forms of life there. Either the areas will become too wet and marshy for the creatures of that area to live, or they will become too dry. Dryness will also increase the risk of forest fires. Of late, we've heard and read of huge blazes which race through forests in tropical countries like Indonesia and Malaysia, and sometimes even in the US. These forest fires themselves send up carbon dioxide into the atmosphere, contributing to the greenhouse effect.

As the forest cover gets reduced, less carbon dioxide is absorbed, so more of it floats up to the atmosphere.

And then there are the chemicals we put into the atmosphere which attack and destroy the protective ozone layer. This means that more heat is being allowed in, and the harmful ultraviolet rays aren't being properly filtered out either.

Scientists say ultraviolet rays lead to a whole lot of health problems, including skin cancer.

Scientists cannot, of course, predict exactly what will happen in the future, because there are too many variables–that means points that might change and so affect the outcome. But based on existing facts, they can make a pretty good guess–things are going to get from bad to worse very rapidly.

In all this, the most affected group will be the poor in the developing nations. That's doubly sad, because it's the developed nations which are most responsible for the increase in greenhouse gases, not the developing ones. It's also sad because the poor are already at a disadvantage, and if they're going to be hit by famine, flood and health problems, they're only going to be pushed further down.

Equally at risk are the other forms of life that call this Earth their home. We already know Nanuq's problems. Sharing his habitat are other animals like the arctic fox and the snow owl. Their survival is also in danger.

At the opposite end of the Earth live the penguins, the Emperor Penguins and the Fairy Penguins. As the waters become warmer, their life becomes harder and food becomes scarcer. Most importantly, their feathers, which nature carefully designed to regulate body heat, will make them too warm for comfort. In fact, the habitat of the penguins is even more at risk that that of Nanuq and friends, because scientists have found that the ozone layer above the Antarctic has been severely damaged, more so than in other places.

Concerned environmentalists are doing their best to protect the endangered species. The Fairy Penguins which nest on Philip Island in Australia, for instance, are very carefully looked after, and, while tourists can watch and wonder and learn, they aren't allowed to get close to them, talk loudly or even take photographs. But the sad truth is that their numbers are declining, because it's becoming harder for them to survive in a changing environment.

Will our great grandchildren have to watch 'old' movies like *Happy Feet* and marvel at those cute species of birds called penguins which lived about a hundred years ago, just as we watch *Jurassic Park* and *Journey to Big Water* now and are awed by the Terrible Lizards that lived millions of years ago?

Should we wait for The Day After Tomorrow, or can we do something to slow down global warming RIGHT NOW?

Chapter 7 What In The World Is Happening?

Many people all over the world are aware that we need to do something, and do it fast, to slow down global warming.

These people belong to all levels–they are government officials, policy makers, scientists, environmentalists, international organizations and also ordinary people like you and me.

There's a lot that can be done at various levels.

Basically, we need to identify the problem and then go about taking action.

It has been seen that along with the rapidly rising global temperature, the quantity of carbon dioxide content in the atmosphere has also been rising alarmingly. So it is reasonable to conclude that there is a link. And carbon dioxide is being put into the atmosphere by the increased burning of fossil fuels. Fossil fuels are being burnt to provide for man's energy needs. So the best thing to do would be to cut down energy consumption and find other means of generating energy as well.

Many governments are working towards this. For one, they're looking at alternative sources of energy, which don't require the burning of fossil fuels like coal and petroleum, and are renewable as well. This means that these sources won't run out as easily as coal or oil reserves, which are bound to be used up sooner or later.

Can you think what these alternative sources of energy may be? Wind and sun, to name just two. The Indian government has a whole department dedicated to non-conventional energy sources. This department studies and encourages the use of such resources to generate power. In some places in Tamil Nadu, large tracts of land are covered with windmills. The whirling blades harness the energy of the wind and it is stored for lighting and other purposes. As yet, this source of energy isn't producing enough to replace other sources of power on a large scale, but technologists are working to improve the output.

Then there is solar power. In many places in India, you will see some extra fittings on rooftops, which are actually solar panels which make use of the heat of the sun. This method, like wind energy, is quite cheap, and the energy produced in this way can be stored for short periods too. In Bangalore for instance, where the need for hot water is high because of its cool climate, solar heaters are very common.

There is also a lot of research being conducted into bio-fuel–fuel that is generated from plants. Jatropha is one such plant, and the government is encouraging its cultivation. Many farmers are turning from traditional crops to jatropha, because of its exciting possibilities as a source of fuel. This is called bio-diesel, and recently, a British firm has come forward to produce it in a cheaper way. It is looking at starting jatropha cultivation in many parts of the world, with India being a major producer. The government is also funding studies on how petrol and diesel can be mixed with other substances to lower harmful emissions and so reduce carbon dioxide release.

Vehicles are a major source of pollution. You have seen cars, buses or lorries letting out evil-smelling black smoke from their exhaust pipes at one time or another. Such sights were very common not very long ago, but now, the authorities are insisting on periodic pollution control tests for vehicles. They have to be certified to be non-polluting before they're allowed on roads. Also, many governments, including the developed nations, have asked car manufacturers to undertake studies and find ways of making vehicles that roll out from their factories less harmful to the environment. Some parts have had to be replaced, others modified. The awareness is there, and so solutions are always possible.

Apart from this, governments have admitted that factories are sending up harmful gases into the atmosphere, and they need to be controlled. These gases are either increasing the greenhouse effect or destroying the protective ozone layer.

Many countries have laws specifying the maximum amount of pollutants that factories can generate. Periodic tests are carried out and licences can be either denied or withdrawn if they don't follow rules. That makes people careful about the processes they follow.

The USA has a Clean Air Act which makes it compulsory to limit the release of harmful substances like volatile organic compounds or VOCs and chlorofluorocarbons or CFCs. The latter are particularly harmful to the ozone layer. In fact, scientists and environmentalists report that the hole in the ozone layer over the Antarctic has grown wider and wider, and now is almost the size of the entire North American continent! Can you imagine how much harmful heat is being let in? Time to take action and save the penguins for our grandchildren, isn't it?

Companies in the US will soon have to follow rules making it compulsory to warn people about the harm their products could cause the environment. They will have to stick labels on their stuff saying this item contains such-and-such a chemical, which is harmful to the environment. It is hoped that responsible people will read the labels and decide not to buy such products, which will force companies to turn to some other business or find substitutes for the harmful substances.

This could work in a positive way too. Companies which have done research and developed processes and products that are NOT harmful to the environment can also stick labels on their stuff saying they don't release

VOCs or CFCs, and are environment-friendly. This means that people will prefer to buy these products, and sales will go up.

In India, authorities are quite aware of the dangers of global warming. There are strict pollution control laws, and before a factory is given a license to start work, the pollution control officials have to be sure that the processes and materials that are going to be used won't harm the environment.

There's also an increasing interest in organic farming all over the world, in India too. Organic farming is cultivation carried out without using chemical fertilizers, which give out harmful methane and also affect our health. So organic farming has the double advantage of being better for our health and better for the world's health as well. Many supermarkets in the big cities of India now stock and display products with labels saying they're organically cultivated and processed.

Another precaution is to reduce the use of cheap plastics. Plastic carry bags and Styrofoam cups, or disposable cups, are very common today, in India and all over the world. The problem is that these things aren't bio-degradable, which means that they will not decay and mix into the soil, unlike other material such as jute and paper.

Plastic waste forms a major chunk of garbage, and this garbage is usually disposed of in landfills. The waste then remains on the earth, gradually poisoning land and air. If garbage is disposed of by burning, plastic and Styrofoam release an alarming quantity of substances that increase global warming and hit human health in other ways too. So governments around the world are trying to reduce the use of plastics.

India is no exception. Some states have banned the use of plastic carry bags, and shoppers come away with paper bags of all sorts, from the cone, quickly twisted, to hold groundnuts hot from the pan, to smart bags, given out in high-class stores. Disposable plates made of processed plant material are also becoming fashion statements, which environmentalists gladly encourage. A company in Taiwan recently came up with dinner plates made of wheat, so you can eat your place after your dinner! Wasn't that very smart?

Governments are passing laws, and it is up to the citizens of the world to observe these rules.

In India and abroad, in order to create awareness about the seriousness of the problem and ensure that ordinary people follow the rules, officials sometimes rope in celebrities like actors and sportstars to convey the message. Often, these personalities feel very strongly about the issue, and talk passionately on the subject, which makes a big impact on people.

In Chennai, popular film star Madhavan spoke on the subject of global warming, and used the common or house sparrow to show how various species are vanishing because of changing ecological conditions, which in turn are affected by the way we humans live. Have you seen sparrows recently? They used to live in flocks near houses and sheds, nesting in window boxes and lamp holders and even the cups of ceiling fans. But now they're a rare sight.

If it's become hard to spot a common sparrow, think how much harder it will be to catch sight of Nanuq or his friends.

Governments are doing a lot to slow down global warming. They're doing it individually and collectively too. Many of them have been holding discussions at various places around the globe, on ways and means to reduce global warming and protect the environment.

Organised efforts began as early as 1992, when world leaders met at Rio de Janeiro and vowed to protect the environment by reducing greenhouse gas emissions. The United Nations Framework Convention on Climate Change was signed by as many as 154 countries, and was welcomed as a major step forward.

Since then, efforts have been continuously made to control greenhouse gases. Though international environmental organizations like Greenpeace have been battling to make developed nations acknowledge their responsibilities, it has been a very tough task.

The first important breakthrough was achieved in Kyoto, Japan in 1997. A protocol or agreement was signed here, at the end of long-drawn discussions. At Kyoto, many developed nations promised to take steps to reduce by a certain level, the various greenhouse gases emitted by them between 2008 and 2012. A different target was fixed for each country depending on its industrial and economic levels.

Unfortunately, many nations, unlike the UK and Germany, had failed to honour their promises made in the earlier UN Framework Convention, and the Kyoto Protocol also ran into trouble. Russia agreed to join later, but the US pulled out. President George W Bush said in 2001 that the Kyoto Treaty would harm America's interests, and so the USA didn't want to be party to it.

The other nations which were party to the treaty held meetings, and made some progress, but were not confident of making any great difference without the cooperation of the US.

Campaigners against global warming received a real boost when the Nobel Prize for Peace in 2007 went jointly to Al Gore and the Intergovernmental Panel on Climate Change (IPCC), a United Nations body. Al Gore, who was Vice President of USA under Bill Clinton, and the IPCC have been seriously fighting against global warming, carrying out intense publicity on the effects and dangers of neglecting the environment for short-term gains.

Gore won an Oscar for his documentary film called *An Inconvenient Truth* which shows how human activities are affecting the Earth's natural environment. The documentary is proof of his fight against global warming.

The IPCC, set up in 1988 by the World Meteorological

Organization and the United Nations Environment Programme, uses the services of over 2,000 experts. It collects and studies data from other organizations working on environment and climate, and prepares its own reports.

Did you know that the IPCC is headed by an Indian? Rajendra Pachauri was born in Nainital, a lovely hill station in North India. He must have admired the beauty of the snow-capped Himalayas as a boy, and enjoyed winter sports too. As a man, he is working to save the world from getting over-heated, and melting the ice everywhere.

The IPCC has warned in very strong terms that global warming is 'unequivocal'. That means that there can be no argument about it. As this book was being written, the IPCC released a report in Spain, saying it was a 'final warning to humanity'. The report said that it was now sure that the Earth's temperature would go up 3.6 degree F and put a staggering 30 per cent of the world's wildlife resources at risk. It will also pose a threat to millions of people living in coastal areas, as these places face the threat of flooding. Think back to your world-on-a-plate experiment.

Most scary of all, the report says that time is running out for us. If we don't reverse the rise of the mercury in the barometer by 2015, it will be too late to prevent the worst disasters from hitting us. 'What we will do in the next two, three years will determine our future. This is the defining challenge of our age,' said Pachauri.

In contrast to the many people and groups who are warning the world about the consequences of global warming and fighting to slow it down are organisations like Accu-Weather Inc., a business-trade body, which have been working to prove that global warming isn't really related to human activity, and argue that no curbs need to be imposed on industry and other fields.

Not all businesses and industry houses feel that it is safe for the world to continue in its present trend. Some big corporate houses support the campaigners against global warming, but the sad truth is that there's a long way to go before we can sit back and say with satisfaction that we've managed to save Nanuq's home, and ours too.

You see, the developed nations have to choose between present prosperity and long-term gain, and developing nations have to decide whether to make the most of carbon economy–pursuing activities that will strengthen their economy but also increase the carbon dioxide content in the atmosphere. It's a hard choice for them to make, because the things that the anti-global warming campaigners are telling the world are 'Inconvenient Truths', like the title of Al Gore's documentary.

What is India's position?

Chapter 8 Where In The World Is India Today?

We ended the last chapter by wondering about India's stand on the issue of global warming.

At Risk, to put it in two words.

Our coastlines are changing, as satellite pictures show. Many little islands have already vanished, or are too waterlogged to be habitable. People living on them have moved inland, adding to pressure on the rest of the country's living area.

Our climate is changing. A few places are seeing snow for the first time in living memory. Others, like Cherapunji, which we learnt from GK books was the wettest place in the world, are no longer receiving high amounts of rainfall. Cherapunji's rain patterns are definitely different now. Other places which are not equipped to cope with huge amounts of water are being battered by heavy rains.

Apart from these events of unusual weather in many places, the country as a whole has been experiencing erratic climate–rain outside the regular rainy seasons, hotter than average summers, colder than average winters, due to which crop patterns are changing too.

Then there are the rivers. The Ganga, India's most sacred river, is already in danger because of pollution. But scientists now say that the shrinking Himalayan ice will mean that less and less fresh water will flow into the river over the years.

As a developing nation, India isn't called upon to impose any strict rules under the Kyoto Protocol.

The government faces some tough choices. It needs to push ahead with industrialization if the country is to continue to grow, and poverty is to be reduced. But more industries mean greater threat to the environment, and officials are well aware of the dangers that this could bring to the country in particular and the world as a whole.

Prime Minister Manmohan Singh has committed to taking steps to encourage clean energy as a means of reducing global warming. Committees are working on more efficient use of energy, as we can't afford to cut back on industrialization and thus cut down on energy. Rules to cut down vehicular pollution are also being made stricter.

The government has also started a 'Green India' programme which means increasing forest areas will be undertaken. This will make up for the huge loss of tree cover that happened earlier. Planting more trees means that more carbon-dioxide in the air will be absorbed and replaced with oxygen, and so there will be less carbon dioxide added to the atmosphere.

Most important, the authorities plan to make all-out efforts to explore alternative, renewable sources of energy, like wind, sea and sun, as well as nuclear energy. Even if these non-conventional sources provide energy for domestic lighting and heating purposes in pockets, it will add up to a lot of saving as regards emission of greenhouse gases.

Some countries, notably Japan, have promised to help us in the fight against this problem.

On the whole, the people of India are aware of the dangers of Global Warming, and are acting responsibly.

The vast majority of us Indians may not have hopes of ever seeing polar bears in the wild, not because we fear they'll vanish in the near future, but because we just won't be able to afford the expensive trip to Nanuq's homeland. But right here, in our own country, we are already missing the butterflies and bees which pollinate and propagate plants, there aren't as many of them to be seen as before, because there's less greenery around.

We've seen how the common sparrow isn't so common any more. People in hot Chennai might have been thrilled to watch a hailstorm, because they'd never seen one before, but it would have set off alarm bells in many minds, because people would have instinctively realized that was a deviation from pattern, and could spell big trouble.

So we're sitting up and taking notice. But things need to be speeded up, and every little bit counts.

Chapter 9

That's Cool!

Hey kids! McDonald's is giving Big Macs at half price!!! Come get it quick!

Wow!! What an offer, you think.

Oh, wait a minute, there're some conditions. You need to promise to do something first. . . .

What?

Nothing too difficult. You just have to pick a few ways in which you can save energy and resources and promise to follow them.

Like what, for instance?

You could promise to cut shower time by a minute, you could promise to use your car less often, you could promise to turn down the heater or the air-conditioning, simple things like that.

Oh, is that all? No problem, I'll promise anything you like. Just lead me to the Big Mac at half-price, and make that order two.

That's not a dream which some Global Warming campaigner is enjoying.

It actually happened. In September 2007, the McDonald's unit in Japan offered an almost 50 per cent discount on the price of a Big Mac to people willing to commit themselves to various ways of reducing Global Warming. To get the discount, they had to download a form from the Japanese Environment Ministry site, and tick boxes agreeing to do various things. The government website crashed because there was such a rush on the site!

Don't you think you'd want to commit yourself to some of these simple measures if you are offered a chance?

McDonald's is only one of about 80 corporate houses in Japan which have come out with various schemes to draw the public into the fight against Global Warming.

Such schemes increase public awareness. But in the long run, only whole-hearted commitment from each of us can win the day for Planet Earth.

We need to keep in mind that Global Warming shoots up by the increasing use of energy, so we need to reduce our use of power–electricity, as well as fuel. We also need to conserve our resources, because less waste means less need to produce more.

So here are some of the things that you and I can do, to make a difference:

First of all, SWITCH IT OFF. Don't keep your electrical equipment on standby. When you're not using your computer, switch it off. When you go out of the room, switch off the lights and fans, even if you're planning to come back in five minutes. Switch the TV off completely when you've finished watching. Don't just turn it off with the remote, and keep it on standby.

Other ways in which you can save on power:

Use energy-efficient bulbs–there are plenty of choices available in the market–instead of the conventional high-consumption bulbs.

Don't use multiple plugs more than you can help–they're those big plugs with many points in them, which allow you to plug in several devices at one electrical point. These waste power.

Cut down your use of the air-conditioner, wear cooler clothes, keep your room well ventilated. Similarly, in cold weather conditions, put on an extra sweater or a muffler instead of turning up the heater.

When you buy new electrical equipment, find out about energy consumption, and choose gadgets which need less power.

When you're running the washing machine, see that you put in a full load each time, instead of doing little bits every now and then, which means more power and water are used.

All these measures will cut down on the electricity bill and your parents will be pleased, while it also means that less carbon-dioxide is released into the atmosphere.

There are also ways in which you can save on petrol or diesel.

If your parents are thinking of getting a car or any other vehicle, talk to them about pollution norms and emissions, and get them to go for an energy efficient, pollution-free model.

If you already have a vehicle, use it only if you have to. Walk wherever you can. Or use the public transport whenever possible. Car pools (more people using one car on every trip) are another good option. Get a bicycle– it's good exercise, and needs only the power of your feet on the pedals. All this means less fuel is used per person.

And fuel saved is less of greenhouse gas emissions.

Next, we come to resources. When you're using water, be careful not to waste it. When you're brushing your teeth, don't keep the tap running the whole time. Reduce the water you use for your bath.

Recycle as much as you can. Ask your mom to keep the water she uses to rinse vegetables in, and use that for the garden. Paper can be easily recycled–use old envelopes and the back of fliers as note-pads and paper for rough work.

Don't waste food. It's precious. Serve yourself only as much or as little as you need.

Ask your parents to buy as much fresh food as possible, because frozen food takes a lot of energy to produce and preserve.

Separate organic waste from non-biodegradable waste, and use the organic waste as compost, instead of harmful chemical fertilisers.

Plant a tree, or at least a plant. Make a little garden for yourself on your balcony if you're living in a flat. Remember, plants and trees absorb carbon dioxide and give out oxygen. It's the least we can do to make up for the harm we're doing the environment by indulging in activities that generate more greenhouse gases.

You may wonder how such little acts can prevent or even slow down Global Warming. Remember, we have an example in the greenhouse gases. It's the one per cent component of the atmosphere which makes all the difference. So even if you're young, too young to decide on national and international policies, you're not too young to decide to take such simple steps.

And pass on the message. Tell your family, your friends, your classmates, neighbours, everyone you can about global warming, the dangers that it will cause, and the simple ways in which we can help save our world.

Every little bit counts. If we all do our bit, Nanuq's cubs will live to hunt seal and walrus from large, closely-packed ice floes which bump into one another as they move gently in the icy waters of the Arctic Ocean.

Who knows, you may even be able to afford a trip to the North Pole with all the money you're going to save on fuel and resources, and see Nanuq's cubs for yourself. That'll be cool, won't it?

www.ingramcontent.com/pod-product-compliance
Ingram Content Group UK Ltd.
Pitfield, Milton Keynes, MK11 3LW, UK
UKHW040003200726
13854UKWH00001B/16

9 788183 686198